26   25   24   23   22   8   7   6   5   4   3   2   1

LOVED FOREVER

Published by:
Barefoot Publishing

www.publishbarefoot.com

Library of Congress Cataloging-in-Publication Data:
ISBN: 978-1087947770-9

Printed in the United States

Loved forever

Written by:
Mariana Neufeld

Illustrated by:
Monica Ortiz

To Leeland Jase
And all the Mommas who loved enough choose life.

Baby Boy, God has a perfect
plan for you.

Our family is different than some.

You have a mommy who carried you in her tummy—a Tummy Mommy

And a mommy who
waited and prayed for you
in her heart—Me.

Your Tummy Mommy
gave you life...

And then, she gave your Daddy and Me the greatest gift-her boy, **OUR boy,** to love forever.

She loved you very much. And she knew you would be **safe and loved** with Daddy, Me, and your sisters.

You may not have my eyes or my smile,

but from the moment I knew
about you, you had my heart.

I prayed for you, Baby Boy, in my heart like I prayed for your sisters in my tummy.

Yes, our family is different than some, and

You, my boy.

I knew you before I formed you in your mother's womb. Jeremiah 1:5

CPSIA information can be obtained
at www.ICGtesting.com
Printed in the USA
LVHW071124060722
722707LV00040B/808

9 781087 947709